INTRODUCTION TO
THE SECOND EDITION

by JAMES BARR, F.B.A.

Distinguished Professor of Hebrew Bible, Vanderbilt University,
and Regius Professor of Hebrew, Emeritus, Oxford University

THE Preface and Introduction which my father wrote for the original edition of his Diagram was concerned principally with pragmatic questions. He introduced the organization and use of the Diagram and furnished the practical explanations necessary for the use of it by the reader; and along with this he provided a minimal statement of the critical theories implied, such as the existence of the document Q and the use of the symbols M and L for the material peculiar to Matthew and Luke respectively. Into the more general implications for biblical hermeneutics he did not go. Since the time when he wrote (the original publication was in 1938, and his actual composition of the material was some considerable time before that), public interest in hermeneutic questions has greatly increased. Meanwhile the initiative of the publishers, Messrs T. & T. Clark, has made possible the publication of a new edition, and it seems good therefore to add a further Introduction, which will seek to place the question of relations between the three Synoptic Gospels within the full context of modern discussions of interpretation.

One of the main features of the Bible is that it contains a number of passages, or complete books, that are parallel to each other, whether roughly or closely, and that tell the same story or deal with the same matters, but in different ways. In the Hebrew Bible (Old Testament) we have two versions of the Ten Commandments (Exodus 20.2–17 and Deuteronomy 5.6–21). Some of the commands are practically identical as between the two versions but others contain substantial differences. In Hebrew poetry, Psalm 18 is paralleled by another version in 2 Samuel 22, which is closely similar in general but has many differences in detailed wording. Among historical texts, a substantial piece concerning the reign of King Hezekiah is found in two versions, one in 2 Kings 18–20 and the other in Isaiah 36–39.   Most strikingly of all, the Books of Chronicles retell at length the material told in Samuel and Kings. Very often Chronicles uses the exact words of these older books (hardly anyone doubts that Chronicles as a complete work belongs to a much later date); and yet on the other hand at other points it introduces new material, but leaves out aspects that in Samuel and Kings were very significant. Thus, for example, Chronicles omits almost all mention of the reign of Saul apart from his death and likewise omits the chronological data, customary in Kings, concerning the kings of northern Israel.   It omits large portions of the story of David which might seem discreditable, such as his adultery with Bath-sheba, his murder of her husband Uriah, and the series of family feuds and conflicts within his family, including the rape of Tamar, the murder of Amnon, the rebellion of Absalom and its disastrous effects upon David.   It explains that it was Satan (1 Chron. 21.1) who incited David to make a census of the nation, and not God as had been stated in 2 Samuel 24.1.   This story, culminating in an important statement of expiation, is at least retained by Chronicles in full detail, though with further modifications; but the companion story of expiation over the sons of Saul and the Gibeonites, contained in 2 Samuel 21.1–14, is left entirely absent.   Where Samuel/Kings make it clear that David had been told not to attempt the building of the temple and that it was Solomon who undertook its construction, Chronicles has David provide the complete plan for the project (1 Chron. 28.11–19), including the organization of the Levites, temple singers and so on (1 Chron. 23.1–26.28).   Again, Chronicles introduces the repentance of King Manasseh (2 Chron. 33.10–20; contrast the handling of this reign in 2 Kings 21.1–18), and as a whole conveys a very different impression of that story and its theological purport.

Many more examples could be added, but these are sufficient for our purpose.   They show us that, within the Hebrew biblical tradition, it is fairly common for parallel texts to be created, in which an older form has been used by a later writer or writers and has been modified by amplification, omission, alteration of wording and change of position; and that the effect of such modifications was, at least potentially, to alter the historical depiction conveyed by the text or to alter the religious and theological impression created, or both.

The reader should notice therefore that these similarities plus differences between parallel texts are not hypothetical relations, the product of the scholarly imagination: on the contrary, they are there in the texts themselves, there to be seen "synoptically", as soon as one arranges the texts in parallel columns.   The production of passages, or of whole books, in a relation of community and difference that can be studied synoptically is a well-established feature of biblical literature, evidenced by the Bible itself.

A DIAGRAM OF SYNOPTIC RELATIONSHIPS

ALLAN BARR

Second Edition
With a New Introduction by
JAMES BARR

T&T CLARK
EDINBURGH & NEW YORK

T&T CLARK LTD

A Continuum imprint

59 George Street	370 Lexington Avenue
Edinburgh EH2 2LQ	New York 10017–6503
Scotland	USA
www.tandtclark.co.uk	www.continuumbooks.com

First published 1938
This edition 1995
Reprinted 2002

ISBN 0 567 09724 2

British Library Cataloguing-in-Publication Data
A catalogue record for this book is available from the British Library

Typeset by Waverley Typesetters, Galashiels
Manufactured in Great Britain

In the Christian Bible the Gospels are the supreme example. Surely the most venerated of all texts, and practically the sole source for the story of Jesus, they form an absolutely central case for all discussion of interpretation. But they are also the supreme case for the kind of parallelism that invites and requires a synoptic investigation and understanding. To this there is indeed one great exception: the Fourth Gospel, John. For though it tells in a sense the same story, starting (after a theological prologue quite different from anything in the other three Gospels) with John the Baptist and ending with Passion and Resurrection, much of the material contained is of a quite different sort from that found in the other three. The parables which are so characteristic of the latter are mostly unrepresented in John, while John has lengthy discourses of a kind not found in the others. Thus John does not lend itself to a consistent synoptic co-examination with the other three in the way in which the other three lend themselves to co-examination with one another. There are indeed numerous points at which comparison is profitable. Thus in the matter of the order of events, which is an important criterion, John places the expulsion of the money-changers from the temple by Jesus at the very beginning of his story (John 2.13–22), making it the very first event after the original call of the disciples and the wedding in Cana, while all the other three Gospels place it within the last days before Jesus' death (Mark 11.15–19 and parallels), thus making it a part of the climactic story of the Passion. In spite of the existence of such examples, however, it remains true that much Johannine material cannot be profitably correlated with the other Gospels in the way in which the material of the other three can be correlated. At many points at which the same matter is handled, these three have the very words in common to a considerable extent. True "synoptic" study attaches therefore to the three "Synoptic" Gospels of Matthew, Mark and Luke.[1]

For a synoptic study the presentation of the material through a Diagram, as developed by my father, has many great advantages. It has indeed to be complemented with a copy of the full text, since only a full text provides the necessary detail. And the full text is best presented in the form of a Synopsis, which displays the full text of all three Gospels, each in its own sequence. And, needless to say, precise perception of the detail is possible only with the text in Greek. The Synopsis recommended by my father was that of Huck, which originally printed the Greek text but is now available also with the text in English. A more complex edition is that of Aland.[2]

[1] A number of the published Synopses, however (see next note), do include John, but this tends only to make them more complex and difficult to use.

[2] Among Synopses which are currently available we may list:

Huck, A., & Greeven, H., *Synopsis of the First Three Gospels with the Addition of the Johannine Parallels* (13th edition, Tübingen: Mohr, 1981). A modern edition of the traditional Huck Synopsis, in Greek.

Here a note of warning may be sounded, which was not included in writing by my father but was assuredly there in his mind. Alongside the various Synopses that exist, there also exist what are called Harmonies of the Gospels (or other similar title), and some readers may suppose that they are equally useful for the purpose. This is not so. The purpose of a Harmony in many cases, as the name suggests, is to eliminate or harmonize the differences between the Gospels, in order to produce a smoothly-running narrative which appears to comprise all the Gospel material without variation of detail or of chronology. In fact this can be done only by suppressing differences. Where this is done, investigation into the relations between the Gospels is impeded. A Synopsis is not a Harmony but a full presentation of the text of all three Gospels in parallel, and it highlights the differences because it is through them that a deeper knowledge of the Gospels can be attained.

The advantage of the Diagram as a mode of presentation is that it displays very clearly and on one visual plane six things that are highly essential: (a) the relative lengths of a passage as between Gospels (e.g. where Mark has a passage that is also in Matthew and/or Luke, the Marcan version is commonly longer); this is displayed because the Diagram is to the scale of 32 verses to one inch; (b) the extent of material which is found in Mark and also in one or both of the other two Gospels; this is indicated by red; (c) the existence of material which is peculiar to one of the three Gospels; this is indicated by white in Matthew, by yellow in Luke, and by green for the small amount of material peculiar to Mark; (d) the existence of material which is common to Matthew and Luke but absent from Mark; this is indicated by blue; (e) differences in order as between Mark and the other two Gospels, or between Matthew and Luke; these are indicated by lines drawn between one column and another; (f) passages in Mark which are absent from either Matthew or Luke are indicated with a heavy black block at the appropriate side. All this can be quickly seen by the student of the Bible without having to look up references or turn over pages.

The differences in order are a matter of great importance. They are best seen on left and right of the Mark column, where red lines indicate

Throckmorton, B. H., Jr., *Gospel Parallels: A Synopsis of the First Three Gospels* (3rd edn., New York and London: Nelson, 1967). A Synopsis with the English text of RSV, following the 9th edition of the Huck-Lietzmann Synopsis.

Sparks, H. F. D., *A Synopsis of the Four Gospels* (London: Black, 1974).

The Aland Synopsis exists in several forms:

Aland, K., *Synopsis Quattuor Evangeliorum* (Greek only; 13th edition, Stuttgart: Deutsche Bibelgesellschaft, 1985)

Aland, K., *Synopsis of the Four Gospels* (English edition, United Bible Societies, 1982)

Aland, K., *Synopsis of the Four Gospels* (Greek–English edition: German Bible Society, Stuttgart, 1972)

passages in the same order as Mark and black lines indicate passages that are not in Marcan order. Thus, to take one of the most striking instances, Luke places the Rejection at Nazareth (Luke 4.16–30) at a much earlier stage in the story than is indicated by Mark (Mark 6.1–6) and Matthew (Matthew 13.54–58). Where something like this happens it is clearly marked by the black lines crossing over the red ones.

The importance of complementing the Diagram with a full text has been mentioned above, and is to be emphasized in cases of different order. The scale of the Diagram is such that differences in the order of *entire passages* can be indicated, but it is not always possible to mark differences in the order of smaller elements *within* individual passages. Thus the important passage of the Temptations is marked in blue, because it is found in Matthew and Luke (Matthew 4.1–11, Luke 4.1–13) but not in Mark. But space does not permit indication of the difference of order within that passage, in that the three temptations come in a different sequence: the temptation which comes third in Matthew, i.e. the suggestion that the devil would give Jesus all the kingdoms of the world, comes second in Luke.[3] The Diagram, therefore, deals with differences in the order of *passages* on the larger scale, but by its nature cannot indicate small-scale differences of the same kind *within* the passages.

It is the differences in the order of whole passages, however, that are of central importance for the understanding of the Synoptic Gospels. Where passages occur in Mark, the corresponding passages in Matthew and Luke are found in large proportion in the Marcan order (see red lines on either side of the Mark column). Where the order is different, which is less common, we see black lines cutting across these red ones: thus a group from Mark 1–3 come in a different order in Matthew, another group in 5–6. On the Lucan side, the marked difference of order in the rejection of Jesus at Nazareth has been mentioned just above.

Equally clear in the Diagram is the way in which both Matthew and Luke have organized their material which is not also in Mark (white and blue in Matthew, yellow and blue in Luke). Both Gospels begin with a substantial section that is peculiar to that Gospel. Matthew has a large portion (the "Sermon on the Mount", chs. 5–7) which is non-Marcan, another considerable amount, mixed with material shared with Mark, in chs. 10–13, and several other blocks thereafter. Luke has a substantial block from 6.20 to the end of ch. 7 and a very long section from the end of ch. 9 to late in ch. 19 which contains some of the most famous Lucan passages (e.g. the parables of the Good Samaritan and the Prodigal Son) and has only limited portions shared with Mark. Both Matthew and Luke

[3] On this cf. J. Barr, *Escaping from Fundamentalism* (London: SCM, 1984) = *Beyond Fundamentalism* (Philadelphia: Westminster, 1984), p. 79.

had non-Marcan material at the end in the Passion and Resurrection narratives, and Luke especially so. Such arrangements of material are easily traced in the Diagram.

The material (coloured blue) that is common to Matthew and Luke, but absent from Mark, introduces a problem of a different kind, for here scholars have thought of a source or document Q which in itself is no longer extant. The exact character of this grouping of material may be disputed: whether it was a unified (oral or written) document, or a group of different sources, and just how much it contained—whether, for example, all that was in Q is what is represented in the non-Marcan passages common to Matthew and Luke, or whether it contained other elements which are now lost. Most of it consists of *sayings* of Jesus (hence the term Logia sometimes used) but there are some narrative passages also. Some have sought to resist the idea of Q altogether, and this might lead towards the idea that Luke followed and used Matthew. Such arguments may be partly based on textual evidence; but it is likely that they are also motivated by a dislike against any sort of "positing" of hypothetical entities which do not exist as actual texts. Against this it may be replied that hypothetical thinking of exactly this kind is absolutely appropriate and correct for problems of exactly this sort. The very same question recurs in many areas of biblical interpretation other than the Gospels. Here again therefore our study of the Gospels leads us to some of the central hermeneutical questions of the present day.

My father prepared the Diagram with the aim, as he says, of presenting the facts upon the basis of which sources might be delimited; and these facts were, in essence, the percentage of verbal correspondence, verse by verse, between two or three Gospels (see his Introduction, pp. 13–14). The Diagram in itself did not aim to present any one particular solution to "the Synoptic Problem", i.e. the question in what sequence, from what combination of sources, at what dates and through what agency the three existing Gospels had come into existence. Nevertheless his Introduction clearly favoured the sort of thinking represented, on the highest academic level, by B. H. Streeter (*The Four Gospels*, 1924). According to this view, Mark is the earliest of the Gospels and must have been written within about forty years of the death of Jesus. Q was earlier than Mark but was not a Gospel, being mainly a collection of sayings and containing no Passion Narrative. Matthew and Luke independently used Mark and incorporated with it, in very different ways, the Q material and their own peculiar material. When scholars speak of the "Two-Document Hypothesis", they mean that Mark and Q were the two basic documents. Actually, the same could equally well be called the "Four-Document Hypothesis", since the peculiar material of Matthew and of

Luke (M and L) could properly be added.   Some of the reasoning for these positions is concisely stated in the Introduction.[4]

The view thus stated has remained the dominant one but has not been unchallenged in more recent years.   In particular, there has been a revival of support for the older theory of J. J. Griesbach.[5]   According to him, Matthew's Gospel was written first; Luke followed and amended Matthew; and Mark's Gospel was written third, combining the material of both Matthew and Luke.   Another approach has been to retain Marcan priority but to dispense with Q, suggesting that the agreements between Matthew and Luke which formed the basis for the hypothesis of Q could be explained by Luke's following Matthew.[6]   Yet other suggestions have been made and others are likely to emerge from the lively surge of modern hermeneutic discussion.   Nevertheless, as already stated, the view taken by my father has remained and still remains the dominant one.   In any case the material is here displayed in such a manner as to provide the necessary evidence for the discussion of alternative views, in so far as that can be done without going into greater detail than is possible within a diagrammatic presentation.

But it is not my purpose here to argue for one or other solution to the Synoptic Problem, and most users of the Diagram will use it more as a means of becoming acquainted with the nature of the question and less as a step towards solving it.   My present remarks are directed more towards general considerations about the nature of Scripture, considerations which are powerfully forced upon our minds by the nature of these Gospels and which remain valid in whatever way the Synoptic Problem is understood.

At the time of his writing my father thought that "if the priority of Mark is established, it is clear that this Gospel is the main source for our knowledge of the sequence of events in Jesus' Ministry" (below, p. 16). Not everyone today would agree with this.   Even if Mark is the earliest of the four complete Gospels, it was still up to forty years removed in time from the death of Jesus, and thus not in proportion so very distant from the times assigned to Matthew and Luke (dated about A.D. 80–90).   More important, many now think that Mark, even when taken as the earliest complete Gospel, may have been motivated not by an instinct for exact

[4] For a good recent study intended for the general reader, see G. H. Stanton, *The Gospels and Jesus* (Oxford University Press, 1989)

[5] For an energetic argument in favour of the Griesbach hypothesis, see W. R. Farmer, *The Synoptic Problem* (1964); for a balanced evaluation in short space see C. M. Tuckett, "Synoptic Problem", in R. J. Coggins and J. L. Houlden, *A Dictionary of Biblical Interpretation* (London : SCM, 1990), 659–661, and at greater length C. M. Tuckett, *The Revival of the Griesbach Hypothesis* (Cambridge: Cambridge University Press, 1983).

[6] Cf. M. D. Goulder, *Luke. A New Paradigm* (Sheffield: Journal for the Study of the New Testament Supplement Series 20, 1989).

historical reporting but rather by strong theological convictions which have caused him to mould and shape his narrative in the way he has done—just as is the case with Matthew and Luke, and most obviously with John. This leads us on into the area in which the similarities and differences between the Gospels may be most significant: the conceptions of historical and theological truth within the Bible.

One of the surprising things in biblical interpretation is the survival of the idea that the Bible had historical accuracy or "historical reliability", in face of the fact that the Gospels, to Christians the most central and essential of writings, provided the clearest of evidence to the contrary. The explanation may at times be that people normally read only one Gospel at a time; or else, when they do compare them, that they brush aside the differences as if they were insignificant. Individual writers and editors may indeed have aspired to historical accuracy and may have thought that they had achieved it; but the result, when the sources and books are taken together, is such as to show that they did not all succeed in this; and of course it may not have been their concern in the first place. I have already cited above one of the most glaring and obvious cases, namely the placing of the expulsion of the money-changers from the temple at the earliest stage of Jesus' ministry by John. Unless one makes the account a farcical one by arguing that the incident happened twice, there is no alternative to supposing that the writers, or one at least of them, felt free to place the event differently according to their different conceptions of its theological significance, which significance is indicated by the context and narrative position in which the story is placed. And, although Matthew, Mark and Luke are agreed (as against John) in placing the incident at this point, the way in which they integrate it, each to its own context, and the language as used by each, indicate a different theological emphasis for each of them.[7] The different writers attached different values to the Temple. "By sandwiching" the incident "between the two halves of the story of the cursing of the fig-tree" (unlike Matthew, who has both the cursing of the tree and its withering after the incident, and unlike Luke, who has nothing about the fig-tree at all—all of them differences that are clearly marked in the Diagram) "Mark himself evidently intended that each story should illuminate the other".[8] The different setting in the other two Gospels is one of the clues to their different general theological conception.

Other incidents present evidence of a similar kind. In the healing of Jairus's daughter (Matt. 9.18–26; Mark 5.21–43; Luke 8. 40–56) Matthew begins the story with the information that the girl has already died, while in

---

[7] For a discussion see Tuckett, *The Revival of the Griesbach Hypothesis*, ch. II "The Cleansing of the Temple", pp. III–119.

[8] Tuckett, *Revival*, p. II5.

Mark and Luke she is not dead but extremely ill and near to death; in them it is only at a later stage that other persons come with the news that the girl is dead (Mark 5.35; Luke 8.49). It is not possible that both versions are factually accurate.[9] In the story where it is suggested for the sons of Zebedee that they should sit on Jesus' right and left in his glory, in Matthew it is their mother who makes the request on their behalf, in Mark it is they themselves (Matthew 20.20ff., Mark 10.35ff.); Luke does not have the story at all, but one phrase from it is found at an earlier point (Luke 12.50) and the following part of the unit is found far later, in the Passion Narrative and thus in a quite different context (Matthew 20.24ff., Mark 10.41ff., but Luke 22.24ff.; in the Diagram notice black block on the right side of the Mark column at this point, and broken black line across to the later parallel in Luke).

Differences of this kind are numerous, and it should not be thought that they present a difficulty for the appreciation of the Gospels. On the contrary, they are part of the very nature of the Gospels. They are a difficulty only for the conception that complete historical accuracy, "historical reliability" or the like, represents correctly the mode of truth possessed by the Gospels. Where detailed historical reliability is insisted on, the only effect will be to prove that the Gospels are *not* historically reliable. A belief in the *general* trustworthiness of the Gospels, in the sense that the life and teaching of Jesus is adequately conveyed by them and that their theological interpretation of them is authoritative for Christianity, can be sustained only when the insistence on detailed factual accuracy is abandoned. Accurate registration of facts cannot be the mode of truth with which the Gospels operate.

For one of the main effects of synoptic study is to indicate that the relations between the Gospels are *literary* relations. The writers are not to be envisaged on the analogy of three witnesses to a motor accident, who see the same event but remember it and describe it in three different ways. The analogy is entirely false. Some of the Gospel writers were certainly not eye-witnesses; very likely, none of them were. They were, at least in part, persons who were dealing with a story *that already existed in writing*, one which they deliberately and consciously took it in hand at one point to use word for word, at another to modify, to abbreviate, to delete, or to enlarge and supplement. They were independent thinkers who emphasized different aspects of a great common tradition and used the diversity of the Gospel material to express these in their different communities and contexts.

Thus they give different versions of events and speeches and different delineations of the theological problems, different modes of use of the

---

[9] See discussion in J. Barr, *Escaping from Fundamentalism* (London: SCM, 1984) = *Beyond Fundamentalism* (Philadelphia: Westminster Press, 1984), p. 80.

Old Testament,[10] different Christologies and different pictures of Jesus. The modern scholar tends to read the Gospels as complete narratives, but in doing so he or she finds understanding through the ways in which older materials—oral traditions, earlier Gospels, quotations from the Old Testament, documents no longer extant—all alike have been moulded into a new entirety. But this sort of understanding would not have come to be, would not have been possible, but for the interest of generations in the Synoptic Problem and the identification of Gospel origins, sources, dates and modes of combination. The small-scale differences at particular points, some of which, as already mentioned, are too small in scale to be made visible in the Diagram, have to be correlated with the large-scale differences between the complete Gospels; between them however there stand the medium-scale differences, which are essential for the understanding of both, and these are made admirably visible in the Diagram.

[10] For a major recent study see D. A. Carson and H. G. M. Williamson, *It is written: Scripture Citing Scripture* (Cambridge: Cambridge University Press, 1988), which includes chapters on each of the four Gospels, along with other subjects.

A DIAGRAM OF SYNOPTIC RELATIONSHIPS

PREFACE

THE Diagram has been designed to assist the reader of the Synoptic Gospels by giving an accurate presentation of their relationships in a single conspectus, and to enable the student's eye by the use of line and colour to contribute to his understanding of Synoptic questions both in their outline and in their details. While the work is based upon a minute study of the Greek text and a knowledge of Greek is required for a thorough investigation of these relationships, the reader of the English New Testament will be able to use the Diagram for a general survey of the structure and sources of the Gospels and for such detailed study as the comparison of passages in a translation permits. The Greek text adopted in the preparation of the Diagram is approximately that underlying the English Revised Version, but one or two verses of doubtful validity are represented in the Diagram in order to show their affinities.

The Gospels are represented by columns, drawn to such a scale that the relationships even of the individual verses can be indicated. Parallel passages are shown in the same colour, and are connected by lines or printed references between the columns. Colour is also used to distinguish between close and distant resemblances of parallels, a matter of great importance in the material common to Matthew and Luke and in certain parts of Luke related to Mark. Matthew is twice represented, so that its relation to Mark is shown in one column, while the material for the study of Q is conveniently collected between the other column representing Matthew and that representing Luke. All doublets which appear to have a bearing on Synoptic comparison are noted with their parallels at the appropriate places alongside each of the columns.

It has been my aim to apply objective principles in determining parallels, and chiefly that of the proportion of verbal correspondence between passages, combined in some cases with consideration of context. The Diagram therefore does not profess to delimit sources, either by way of inclusion or exclusion, but to present the facts on which such delimitation may proceed. I have, however, made use of doublets in Matthew and Luke to distinguish between similar Marcan and non-Marcan passages in these Gospels.

The beginner in Synoptic studies is enabled by the devices of the Diagram to see at a glance the relative length of the three Gospels, the large proportion of Marcan matter included in the other Gospels, their omissions of Marcan sections, their adherence to or deviation from Marcan order, the distribution of Marcan matter in Matthew and Luke, the extent and connection of non-Marcan matter in Matthew and Luke, the proportion and distribution of matter peculiar to each Gospel, and so on. And it is hoped that sufficient detail is provided in the Diagram to make it permanently useful to the more advanced student, for whom it will illuminate special studies such as that on the theory of Proto-Luke and provide a work of reference for all Synoptic studies.

A brief survey of the Synoptic Problem is combined with the directions given for the use of the Diagram. The survey has been drawn up to aid especially those students who are using the Diagram without the guidance of a teacher or a textbook on the Synoptic Problem.

In the preparation of this Diagram I have consulted the works of many writers on the Synoptic Gospels, and I can make only a general acknowledgement of my indebtedness to them. I wish, however, to mention particularly Huck's *Synopse der drei ersten Evangelien*, in which the Greek text is arranged in a form indispensable for a work of this kind.

My warm thanks are due to Prof. G. H. C. Macgregor, D.Litt., D.D., and Prof. Wm. Manson, D.D., for helpful suggestions, and to Rev. A. Morton Price, B.D., for valuable assistance kindly given in the correction of the proofs.

ALLAN BARR

EDINBURGH 14*th February* 1938.

In a succession of reprints some improvements have been made in the details of the Diagram. For the present impression the pages of Introduction have been revised in the light of recent discussion.

January, 1976   A.B.

INTRODUCTION

A BRIEF SURVEY OF THE SYNOPTIC PROBLEM

WITH DIRECTIONS FOR THE USE OF THE DIAGRAM

THE three Gospels usually distinguished by the titles "according to St. Matthew, St. Mark, St. Luke", are called Synoptic, because they present in a large measure a common view of the life of Jesus. For a knowledge of their sources, authorship and historical value we are almost wholly dependent upon a comparative study of the Gospels themselves. The Diagram is designed to aid such comparison. It presents a *general* survey of Synoptic relations. Itself the product of a close examination of the texts, it should be used in conjunction with detailed study of the Gospels, the student referring to the Diagram from time to time in order to ascertain the relation of any passage under study to the whole Synoptic material. It is a great advantage to have an edition of the Gospels (best in Greek) in which they are arranged in parallel columns, and to mark off in the text the similar and dissimilar elements in them by a system of underlining.

MATTHEW, MARK AND LUKE.—Besides indicating chapter and verse positions the columns of the Diagram show divisions of the subject-matter, corresponding to the units of narrative, etc. (pericopae) of which the Gospels are composed, but in some cases adjusted in length for convenience of Synoptic comparison. These divisions are here called "sections". The Diagram indicates by red colour the sections in the three Gospels in which both Matthew and Luke, or one of them, show considerable verbal correspondence with Mark. It will be seen that almost the whole of the Marcan material is incorporated in one or both of the other Gospels. Of Mark's 662 verses 609 are represented as having parallels in Matthew. In the case of Luke, figures are less definite. The Diagram shows 357 verses of Mark's closely paralleled in Luke, but in addition, some 95 verses of Mark are represented in the sections (chiefly those shown in red and yellow) where Luke is apparently combining Marcan with other material, and where a lower degree of verbal correspondence with Mark is found. In the sections indicated in red,

more than half, on an average, of the *actual words* used are found in both
Matthew and Mark or both Luke and Mark.   There is a somewhat lower
degree of correspondence if account is taken of the *order* of shared words,
and a higher degree if equivalent expressions are considered.   Especially
in their record of the words used by Jesus and others the three Gospels
tend to coincide.   The degree of verbal correspondence is sufficient to
prove literary dependence in one direction or another; at the same time
the variations of the evangelists in their common material indicate their
freedom in the editorial (redactional) handling of the traditions.   A glance
at the Diagram will show that much of the Marcan material is condensed
in Matthew and Luke.   609 verses of Mark are represented by 523 in
Matthew and 357 verses of Mark by 325 in Luke.   The long-prevailing
view that Mark was an abbreviator of Matthew (or Luke) cannot be
maintained in respect of their common material, nor is it easy to explain
why Mark, if dependent upon Matthew and Luke, should expand the
portions he selects for inclusion, and yet omit so much valuable material
from these Gospels.   Only about 30 verses of Mark have no parallel either
in Matthew or Luke.   A few of these, as in 9, 15f., 21ff., are merely
descriptive expansions of the narrative—a common feature of Mark—
which here happen to extend over a verse or two.   Mk. 7, 31–37 corresponds
at some points to Matt. 15, 29–31.

The student should pay great attention to the order (sequence) of the
Marcan material in Matthew and Luke.   This is indicated in the Diagram
by connecting lines between columns A, B and C.   Wherever two of these
lines cross, a deviation from the order of Mark is indicated.   It will be
seen that in no case do Matthew and Luke agree in departing from the
order of Mark.   In Matthew the transpositions chiefly affect chaps. 4, 8, 9
and 10; in Luke a detailed study of the Passion-narrative of chaps. 22, 23,
will reveal a number of minor differences of order in addition to those
shown in the Diagram.   Luke also places a number of distant parallels to
sections of Mark in a non-Marcan context; these are connected by broken
lines in the Diagram.   On the assumption of the priority of Mark, the
Diagram indicates by black connecting lines the passages that seem most
likely to have been moved from the Marcan order in these transpositions.

The most widely accepted conclusion is that Matthew and Luke used
a writing substantially the same as our Mark as one of their sources.   This
view is chiefly based upon the verbal correspondence, agreement in order,
and the details of the Gospels when compared, but on none of these in
isolation from the others.   Theoretically, mere agreement in wording and
order would admit of an opinion (long held and still occasionally
advocated) that Mark was composed by drawing from Matthew and Luke.
The student must test this and other hypotheses in view of the additional
material of Matthew and Luke and the interests and methods of each of
the evangelists as seen in their own Gospels.   With regard to order, the

arrangement of Matthew's and Luke's material at special points (e.g. in Matt. chaps. 3–10) must be studied in relation to the principles of arrangement (in word-order, sentences and sections) shown throughout these Gospels. This may well be decisively in favour of the priority of Mark.

When the three Gospels are compared in detail many of the departures of Matthew and Luke from Mark can be explained as tending to improve harsh and ungrammatical phrases of Mark, to remove redundancies and unessential matter or to heighten expressions of reverence for Jesus (e.g. Mk. 13, 19; 1, 32; 2, 25; 6, 17–29; 4, 38; 6, 5, 6 and parallels). The preservation of the original Aramaic words of Jesus is another sign that Mark is primitive (e.g. 5, 41; 7, 34; 15, 34). Minor agreements of Matthew and Luke against Mark seem to conflict with this view. They may be accounted for by assimilation in the early history of the text, coincidence in the emendation of Mark or the overlapping of Mark and other sources used by Matthew and Luke. Some scholars hold the view that Luke was acquainted with and made limited use of Matthew's Gospel. Explanations can be suggested, if not proved, for Luke's omission of considerable portions of Mark (as indicated at the side of column B).

MATTHEW AND LUKE.—Matthew and Luke show agreement in some of their non-Marcan material. This is coloured blue in the Diagram, and the relevant facts are presented in columns C and D. There is every grade of correspondence from exact identity to agreement in scattered words. In the Diagram, 171 verses of Matthew are represented as closely parallel to 151 of Luke, and 90 of Matthew as more distantly corresponding to 94 of Luke. The evidence points to the use by Matthew and Luke of another written Greek source, to which the symbol Q (German, *Quelle*, Source) or the title Logia (Sayings) is usually given. It is a hypothetical document, and it is impossible to reconstruct it with certainty. The student, however, should go as far as he can towards ascertaining its contents. As Matthew and Luke each omit part of Mark, so they each probably omit part of Q, some of which may be lost altogether, and some may appear among the material peculiar to Matthew and Luke. On the other hand, some of their more distantly related passages (e.g. Matt. 25, 14–30, Luke 19, 11–27) may have come not from Q but from two different sources to the evangelists. The Q material occurs in very different order in the two Gospels, a fact which is no doubt partly due to Matthew's method of fitting all his material into the Marcan outline; but a skeleton order of Q may be seen in the sections occurring in similar sequence in the two Gospels and indicated by connecting lines between columns C and D in the Diagram. The question of the over-lapping of Mark and Q is very important. It is shown by the frequent occurrence in Matthew and Luke of doublets, chiefly short sayings, usually once in a Marcan and once in a non-Marcan context in the same Gospel.

(These and their parallels are noted alongside the columns). Differences of wording between the members of a doublet (seen esp. in Luke) suggest different sources. There is also clearly overlapping in Matthew's and Luke's parallels to Mark 1, 7, 8, 12, 13; 3, 22–30, and other passages. Some short passages which have Marcan affinities (e.g. Matt. 13, 31, 32, Luke 13, 18, 19) may owe more to Q than to Mark. If Mark and Q are independent, such common elements come from traditions earlier than either of them. The variation in the degree of correspondence in the Q sections presents a difficulty. Yet the cases of low correspondence would be matched in Matthew and Luke if they were compared directly, without reference to Mark, in their Marcan material, and in some of the passages an overlapping of Q and other sources may reasonably be offered as an explanation of their difference (cf. Matt. 5, 3–12, Luke 6, 20–26). Some Q sections (e.g. Matt 6, 25–34, 11, 7–19; Luke 12, 22–31, 7, 24–35) show very close correspondence sustained over several verses. Most of the Q material consists of the teaching of Jesus, but some narrative passages are included (e.g. Matt. 8, 5–13, Luke 7, 1–10). It is most unlikely that Q contained a narrative of the Passion; otherwise the presence of common non-Marcan material in Matt. chaps. 26, 27, Luke chaps. 22, 23 would be expected. So Q should not be reckoned as an early Gospel. Q may be confidently assigned to a somewhat earlier date than Mark, which must have been written within about forty years of the death of Jesus. Recognition of Mark and Q as the principal sources constitutes the "two-document theory" of Synoptic origins.

MARK.—If the priority of Mark is established, it is clear that this Gospel is the main source for our knowledge of the sequence of events in Jesus' Ministry. The arrangement in some places is topical rather than chronological, but the narrative hinges on certain great events (e.g. Mark 1, 9–11; 3, 13–19; 8, 27–33; 9, 2–8; 11, 1–10; 14, 22–25) which reveal the nature of Jesus' Messianic vocation. The special characteristics of Mark, his vivid realism in narrative, his portrait of Jesus as at once human and unique in supernatural endowment, and the prominence he gives to Jesus' suffering and death, are brought out by a comparative study of Mark with Matthew and Luke.

MATTHEW.—When the Marcan and Q material is subtracted from Matthew, 282 verses peculiar to this Gospel (as shown in white in the Diagram) of the total of 1069 verses remain, in addition to an indefinite proportion of the 93 verses of the mixed sections (red and white, blue and white). These are not necessarily derived from one source only, but they reveal the characteristic interests of the evangelist. The question whether part of this material is based upon another written source is answered in the affirmative by some scholars, who hold the view that Matthew used a collection of sayings (symbol M) circulating in Jerusalem and showing a strong interest in Jesus' attitude to the Jewish Law. Perhaps this view lies beyond the range of conclusive proof, but the student will find this and other interests of this Gospel (such as the fulfilment of Old Testament prophecy, Jesus' teaching on the Kingdom of Heaven, life in the "Church") prominent in the matter peculiar to Matthew. It is important to observe his careful arrangement of his material from the various sources in appropriate contexts of Mark. It is his method of collecting and uniting his material that gives to columns A and D the striped effect in their colouring. Good examples are seen in chaps. 10, 13, 24, 25.

LUKE.—Luke contains even more special material than Matthew. The Diagram shows 491 verses in yellow, in addition to an indefinite proportion of 173 verses of the mixed sections (red and yellow, blue and yellow) out of the 1150 verses of the whole Gospel. L is regularly used as a symbol of this material. A glance at the Diagram shows that Luke's method of combining his sources is very different from that of Matthew. Instead of introducing cognate material from his other sources at numerous points of Mark, Luke, in the greater part of his Gospel, has solid blocks of Marcan material alternating with blocks of combined Q and L material. (Even the few Marcan verses indicated in the Diagram among the latter may well have come not from Mark but from an overlapping source.) This fact, along with Luke's considerable omissions from Mark, his preference for alternatives to Marcan narratives (e.g. Luke 4, 16–30; 5, 1–11; 7, 36–50; 10, 25–28) and other considerations, has led to the disputed Proto-Luke theory. It is held that Q and L had already been combined by Luke or a predecessor in the form of a Gospel covering the whole Ministry from the Baptism to the Resurrection, and that the Marcan sections were incorporated into its scheme, not Q and L into Mark. That Q and L were combined, either before the composition of the Third Gospel or in the act of composing it, is obvious, but whether Q + L in itself formed a continuous Gospel is far from certain. The junctures between Marcan and non-Marcan material throughout Luke should be examined to test the hypothesis that the Marcan sections are fitted into an already existent framework. Opinions differ as to the extent of Luke's dependence upon Mark in the Passion-narrative. In the Diagram, the verses of Mark most clearly used in the *mixed* sections of Luke's Passion-narrative are shown at the right of column B. If the Proto-Luke theory were confirmed, it would involve an early date for L. Both Matthew and Luke, as we have them, are usually assigned to a date about A.D. 80–90. The special characteristics of Luke, such as his emphasis on Jesus' interest in the poor, the sinful, the outcasts and women, and on the universality of the Gospel message, are brought out by a study of Luke's special material and his treatment of Mark and Q.

THE STUDY OF INDIVIDUAL PASSAGES.—If a passage in one of the Gospels is being studied, the student should consult the Diagram to find its setting in the structure of the Gospel and its relation to any parallels in the other Gospels. If a doublet occurs in the passage, the other member of the doublet and the parallels of both in the other Gospels should be collected and compared. In the study of Matthew both columns A and D should be used.

The Fourth Gospel lies outside the scope of the Diagram, but study of that Gospel involves reference at numerous places to the Synoptic framework, and the Diagram provides a convenient means for such comparison.